21st Century
Junior Library

TALKING ABOUT DISABILITY

AnneMarie McClain
and Lacey Hilliard

Topics to Talk About

Published in the United States of America by Cherry Lake Publishing Group
Ann Arbor, Michigan
www.cherrylakepublishing.com

Reading Adviser: Beth Walker Gambro, MS, Ed., Reading Consultant, Yorkville, IL
Book Designer: Jen Wahi

Photo Credits: Cover: © Jaren Jai Wicklund/Shutterstock; page 5: © Manop Boonpeng; page 6: © Peackstock/Shutterstock; page 7: © Ritmoboxer/Dreamstime.com; page 8: Mangkorn Danggura/Shutterstock; page 9 (top): © Ground Picture/Shutterstock; page 9 (bottom left): © Art_Photo/Shutterstock; page 9 (bottom right): © adriaticfoto/Shutterstock; page 10–11: © AnnGaysorn/Shutterstock; page 12 (left): © linear_design/Shutterstock; page 12 (right): © Pixel-Shot/Shutterstock; page 13: © Mengtianhan/Dreamstime.com; page 14: © antoniodiaz/Shutterstock; page 16: © Rawpixel.com/Shutterstock; page 17: © wavebreakmedia/Shutterstock; page 18 (left): ©; page 18 (right): © Dmitry Markov152/Shutterstock; page 19: © MarinaNy/Shutterstock; page 20–21: © Olesia Bilkei/Shutterstock

Library of Congress Cataloging-in-Publication Data

Names: Hilliard, Lacey, author. | McClain, AnneMarie, co-author.
Title: Talking about disability / written by Lacey Hilliard and AnneMarie McClain.
Description: Ann Arbor, Michigan : Cherry Lake Publishing, [2023] | Series: Topics to talk about | Includes bibliographical references and index. | Audience: Grades 2-3 | Summary: "How do we talk about disability? This book breaks down the topic of disability for young readers. Filled with engaging photos and captions, this series opens up opportunities for deeper thought and informed conversation. Guided exploration of topics in 21st Century Junior Library's signature style help readers to Look, Think, Ask Questions, Make Guesses, and Create as they go!"– Provided by publisher.
Identifiers: LCCN 2022039649 | ISBN 9781668919354 (hardcover) | ISBN 9781668920374 (paperback) | ISBN 9781668921708 (ebook) | ISBN 9781668923030 (pdf)
Subjects: LCSH: People with disabilities–Juvenile literature.
Classification: LCC HV1568 .H556 2023 | DDC 362.4–dc23/eng/20220919
LC record available at https://lccn.loc.gov/2022039649

Cherry Lake Publishing would like to acknowledge the work of the Partnership for 21st Century Learning, a network of Battelle for Kids. Please visit http://www.battelleforkids.org/networks/p21 for more information.

Printed in the United States of America
Corporate Graphics

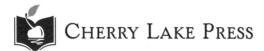

CHERRY LAKE PRESS

CONTENTS

LET'S TALK ABOUT DISABILITY

Some people have what is called a disability. Disability describes why a body or brain might work differently or need different things.

Some people are born with disabilities. Other people develop disabilities later in life. There are many kinds of disabilities. There is nothing wrong with having one. You cannot always tell if someone has a disability by looking at them. Bodies and minds work in all kinds of ways.

In 2019, over 3 million kids in the U.S. had a disability.

5

Only the person with the disability knows exactly how it feels.

People have different ways of living and moving. Disabled people may use equipment, devices, or other things to assist them. Some people have a **service dog** to help guide them. Some may use a **hearing aid**, walk with **crutches** or a **walker**, or use a **wheelchair** to get around.

1 to 3 children out of every 1,000 have some amount of hearing loss.

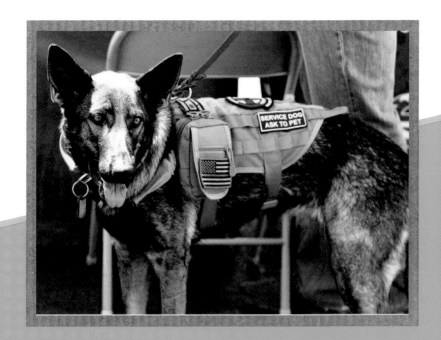

Look!

This dog is specially trained to help people who use support to get around. These types of dogs usually wear vests. When they are wearing their vests, they are working. They go to places where dogs aren't usually allowed because they are special helpers.

You may have seen parking spaces for people with disabilities. Someone may use a vehicle that fits a wheelchair with a ramp or lift. Other disabled people may use these parking spaces for safety. The spaces help people with disabilities easily enter a hospital, school, or store.

People can use resources to help with disabilities. Resources help people manage differences. In school,

resources for disabled kids can be medicine, sign language, or an extra school helper. Resources support and help them learn. Doctors and therapists are also great supports for all people. For disabled people, they can give resources specific to their needs.

All of these supports are ways to make the world **accessible** to people. "Accessible" means people of all abilities have what they need.

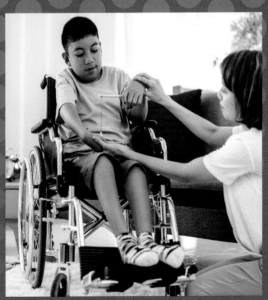

Sometimes disabled kids work with therapists for support.

KIDS AND DISABILITY

You may have a disability. You may know someone with a disability. You can be curious and respectful about their disability. You can ask questions if they say it's okay.

Sometimes places and spaces make it hard for disabled people to get around. Some places and spaces do not include disabled people. Sometimes people seem to forget that bodies and minds can need different things. That's not right.

Make a Guess!

What would the world be like if every place and space was accessible? What might happen? What would it feel like?

Disabled people deserve to be in any space.

Everyone deserves to feel safe and included. Everyone deserves to have what they need.

Think about how to make places work for everyone's needs. Kids can learn about other people's experiences. Kids can help make sure everyone has what they need.

Sometimes concerts or speeches have sign language interpreters. This takes people with hearing disabilities into account.

For some kids with autism, too much noise can be overwhelming. Some kids with autism wear headphones to make things quieter in the classroom.

WHAT'S MOST IMPORTANT TO REMEMBER?

People have all kinds of bodies and minds.
People can need different things. This is all okay!

Think!

Think about your school. In what ways is your school accessible? In what ways is it not?
If you don't know, how can you figure it out?

Disabled people deserve to feel safe and included in any space. Everyone needs to work to make the world equal and fair for everyone.

We can work together to make the world a more fair and equal place for everyone!

We can do so much more to help people with disabilities feel included.

17

REFLECTING ABOUT DISABILITY

Have you ever seen a person with a disability on TV or in a book? If so, did that person have everything they needed? If you have not, what do you think about that? Does that seem fair? Why or why not?

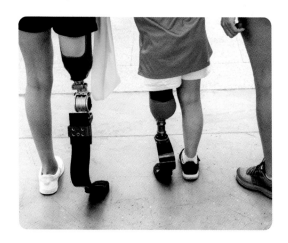

What can you do to make sure kids of all abilities have what they need? What is something you would like grown-ups to do to make sure kids of all abilities have what they need?

Are there places in your community where kids of different abilities may not feel welcome? What could help make these places more welcoming for everyone? What things could you do?

Create!

Draw or write some ideas of things you would like to see in your school to help all kids have what they need. They can be real things or creative inventions or ideas. Talk about why each idea could be helpful.

Ask Questions!

You can ask a grown-up if their workplace is accessible. Think about how to know if everyone has what they need.

Do you have any friends or family members with disabilities? Do they do anything differently than you? What are some things that are the same about you and them?

GLOSSARY

accessible (ak-SEH-suh-buhl) a way to describe when everyone has, or can get, what they need

crutches (CRUHCH-ez) devices used by some disabled people to walk

curious (KYUR-ee-uhs) wanting to know something

disability (dih-suh-BIH-luh-tee) physical or mental condition that might affect what some can do, or how a body or mind works

hearing aid (HEER-ing AYD) small device worn in the ear to help people hear sounds

included (in-KLOO-duhd) made to feel part of a group

resources (ree-SOHR-suhz) things that help people manage

respectful (rih-SPEKT-fuhl) polite and considerate of other people's feelings

service dog (SUHR-vuhs DOG) dog trained to help people with disabilities

walker (WOK-uhr) standing device that helps some disabled people walk

wheelchair (WEEL-chayr) chair on wheels that helps some people get around

LEARN MORE

Book: *Understanding Disability* by various authors
https://cherrylakepublishing.com/shop/show/53069

Book: *We Move Together* by Kelly Fritsch & Anne McGuire
https://www.akpress.org/we-move-together.html

Book: *Just Ask* by Sonia Sotomayer https://www.penguinrandomhouse.com/
books/562056/just-ask-by-sonia-sotomayor-illustrated-by-rafael-lopez

Video: Penfield Children's Center - "Understanding Disabilities" (2018, ~2 mins)
https://www.youtube.com/watch?v=wIAhSeVpQsU

INDEX

ABOUT THE AUTHORS

AnneMarie K. McClain is an educator, researcher, and parent. Her work is about how kids and families can feel good about who they are. She especially loves finding ways to help kids and families feel seen in TV and books.

Lacey J. Hilliard is a college professor, researcher, and parent. Her work is in understanding how grown-ups talk to children about the world around them. She particularly likes hearing what kids have to say about things.